NATURE'S
LIFE
Cycles

The Life Cycle
of an
OPOSSUM

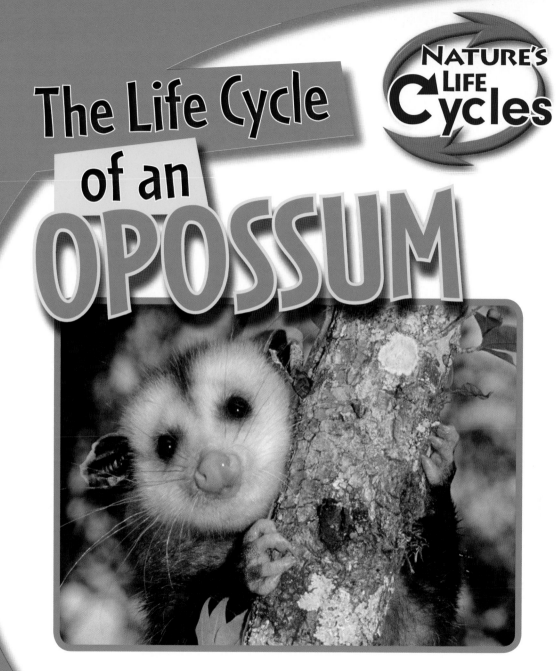

By Barbara M. Linde

Gareth Stevens
Publishing

Please visit our Web site, www.garethstevens.com. For a free color catalog of all our high-quality books, call toll free 1-800-542-2595 or fax 1-877-542-2596.

Library of Congress Cataloging-in-Publication Data

Linde, Barbara M.
 The life cycle of an opossum / Barbara M. Linde.
    p. cm. – (Nature's life cycles)
 Includes index.
 ISBN 978-1-4339-4680-6 (pbk.)
 ISBN 978-1-4339-4681-3 (6-pack)
 ISBN 978-1-4339-4679-0 (library binding)
 1. Opossums—Life cycles—Juvenile literature. I. Title.
 QL737.M34L56 2011
 599.2'76156–dc22

                                                    2010030695

First Edition

Published in 2011 by
Gareth Stevens Publishing
111 East 14th Street, Suite 349
New York, NY 10003

Designer: Daniel Hosek
Editor: Therese Shea

Photo credits: Cover, p. 1 Gail Shumway/Photographer's Choice/Getty Images; pp. 5, 13 (all images), 17, 19, 20, 21 (adult) iStockphoto.com; pp. 7, 9, 11, 21 (young) Shutterstock.com; pp. 9, 21 (baby) Joe McDonald/Visuals Unlimited/Getty Images; p. 15 Steve Maslowski/Visuals Unlimited/Getty Images.

Printed in the United States of America

CPSIA compliance information: Batch #CW11GS: For further information contact Gareth Stevens, New York, New York at 1-800-542-2595.

Contents

Words in the glossary appear in **bold** type the first time they are used in the text.

What Is an Opossum?

An opossum is a **mammal**. It has a long, thin body. Each foot has five toes. One toe on each back foot acts like a thumb. It works with other toes to hold on to things.

An opossum's pointy face is pinkish white, with a pink nose, dark eyes, and whiskers. Its mouth holds 50 sharp teeth. Its large ears and most of its long tail have no hair. The opossum uses its tail to carry things and to help it climb trees.

AWESOME ANIMAL!

The name "opossum" comes from the Algonquian Indian word *pasum*, which means "white animal."

Opossums are also called possums.

A Special Marsupial

An opossum is a **marsupial**. Marsupials are like other mammals except for one big difference. A female marsupial has a pouch where babies grow. Like most marsupials, the opossum has its pouch on its stomach. The pouch is made of skin and fur.

The Virginia opossum is the only marsupial that lives in the wild in North America and Central America. It likes to live in forests and **swamps**. However, some wild opossums have learned to live in cities!

AWESOME ANIMAL!

The Virginia opossum isn't native to the West Coast. However, people took some there, and now opossums live all over the coast!

Opossums live anywhere they can find food.

7

Baby Opossums

Male and female opossums **mate** sometime between January and July each year. After just 12 or 13 days, baby opossums are born. They're only about the size of a fingertip! They're blind and without fur. A female can have up to 20 babies in one **litter**. She may have two litters a year.

The babies aren't ready for the outside world yet. As soon as they're born, they crawl into their mother's pouch. Inside the pouch, they drink their mother's milk.

Baby opossums already have sharp claws!

Hungry Babies

The baby opossums stay in the cozy pouch for 2 or 3 months. They drink milk. They get bigger and stronger. Their fur grows. When they're about 65 days old, their eyes open for the first time.

Now the babies begin to climb out of the pouch. When they're hungry, they go back into the pouch. Sometimes the mother leaves them alone in a den. A den may be a hole in a tree, hollow log, or the ground.

AWESOME ANIMAL!

Opossums have been on Earth for about 80 million years. They were here when dinosaurs existed!

These opossum babies peek out of their den in a tree.

▼

Young Opossums

After 100 days, the young opossums are strong enough to live outside the pouch. However, they're not ready to live on their own. For about 2 more weeks, they stay close to their mother. She takes them for rides on her back. They eat food in their den. Then they start to travel outside the den to find food.

Finally, the young opossums get too heavy to ride on their mother's back. She may already have a new litter in her pouch. It's time for them to go.

Opossums don't see or hear well. They use their good sense of smell to find food.

Young opossums learn how to find food as they ride on their mother's back.

13

Adult Opossums

An opossum grows throughout its life. An adult opossum's body can be from 13 to 20 inches (33 to 51 cm) long. That's about the size of a large cat. The opossum's tail is another 9 to 21 inches (23 to 53 cm) long. An opossum can weigh between 2 and 13 pounds (0.9 and 6 kg). Males usually weigh more than females.

Once they grow up, male opossums live alone. Females sometimes live in groups. In the wild, opossums live up to 4 years. Opossums in zoos live as long as 8 years.

Opossums can hang
from their tail for a
short time. ▶

Night Animals

Opossums are **nocturnal**. They come out at night to eat. Their food includes fruits, vegetables, plants, bugs, small animals, dead animals—even garbage!

Opossums are excellent climbers. Their sharp claws easily hold on to tree trunks. An opossum's tail wraps around tree branches to help it climb.

Most opossums take over the nests or dens of other animals. When an opossum makes its nest, it gathers leaves and grass. Then it wraps its tail around the pile and takes it to the den.

Opossums spend a lot of time in trees.

▼

AWESOME ANIMAL!

An opossum washes itself with its tongue and front feet, just like a cat does.

Playing Dead

Opossums are **prey** for coyotes, foxes, owls, hawks, and other animals. Most of the time, opossums run away or hide. Sometimes they hiss or growl. They don't like to fight.

When a **predator** comes close, the opossum "plays dead." It lies on its side with its eyes either closed, or open and staring. Its tongue flops out of its mouth, and its breathing slows. Even if a predator bites the opossum, it doesn't move! It acts like it's dead until the danger has gone.

AWESOME ANIMAL!

An opossum can play dead for up to 6 hours!

"Playing possum" is a term people use for acting lifeless, just like this opossum.

Lots of Opossums

Opossums seem to be able to live anywhere people live. They even make dens in garages and attics! Sometimes people catch a sick or injured opossum. People with special training can help the opossum. Then they take the opossum back to the wild.

The biggest dangers to opossums come from people. Cars kill many opossums crossing roads. People's pets, such as dogs or large cats, kill opossums, too. In some areas, people hunt opossums for food or for their fur.

The Life Cycle of an Opossum

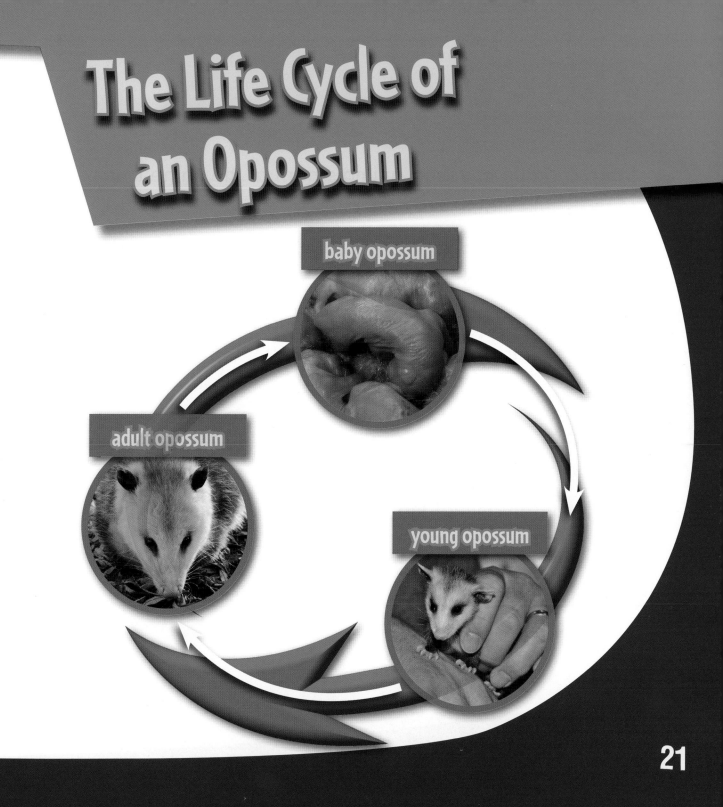

baby opossum

adult opossum

young opossum

Glossary

litter: a group of young animals born at the same time to the same mother

mammal: an animal that has live young and feeds them milk from the mother's body

marsupial: a mammal that has young that grow inside a pouch on the mother's stomach

mate: to come together to make babies

nocturnal: being active at night rather than during the day

predator: an animal that kills animals for food

prey: an animal that is eaten by other animals

swamp: an area covered partly by water

For More Information

Books

Bogue, Gary. *There's an Opossum in My Backyard*. Berkeley, CA: Heyday Books, 2007.

Ripple, William John. *Opossums*. Mankato, MN: Capstone Press, 2006.

Webster, Christine. *Opossums*. New York, NY: Weigl Publishers, 2008.

Web Sites

Opossum

animals.nationalgeographic.com/animals/mammals/opossum.html

Read more about how an opossum hunts for food.

Virginia Opossum

www.biokids.umich.edu/critters/Didelphis_virginiana

See photos of opossums and learn more about their roles in nature.

Index